8/13
2/21

CRINOIDS AND BLASTOIDS

By Susan H. Gray

THE CHILD'S WORLD®
CHANHASSEN, MINNESOTA

The Child's World®

Published in the United States of America by The Child's World®
PO Box 326, Chanhassen, MN 55317-0326
800-599-READ
www.childsworld.com

*Content Adviser:
Brian Huber, PhD,
Curator, Department
of Paleobiology,
Smithsonian
National Museum
of Natural History,
Washington DC*

Photo Credits: Stephen Frink/Corbis: 5; Brandon D. Cole/Corbis: 11; Jeffrey L. Rotman/Corbis: 15; Jonathan Blair/Corbis: 18; Raymond Gehman/Corbis: 24; Denis Scott/Corbis: 25; The Field Museum, Neg #GEO85829c, Photographer John Weinstein: 6; Mike Fredericks: 12, 13; Todd Marshall: 27; Charles Messing/Nova Southeastern University: 19; Laurie O'Keefe/Photo Researchers, Inc.: 4; Kaj R. Svensson/Photo Researchers, Inc.: 7; James L. Amos/Photo Researchers, Inc.: 8; Mark A. Schneider/Photo Researchers, Inc.: 9, 14; Michael Patrick O'Neill/Photo Researchers, Inc.: 17; A. Flowers & L. Newman/Photo Researchers, Inc.: 20, 22; George Lower/Photo Researchers, Inc.: 21; J. Gerard Smith Photographer/Photo Researchers, Inc.: 23.

The Child's World®: Mary Berendes, Publishing Director

Editorial Directions, Inc.: E. Russell Primm, Editorial Director; Pam Rosenberg, Line Editor; Katie Marsico, Associate Editor; Matthew Messbarger, Editorial Assistant; Susan Hindman, Copy Editor; Melissa McDaniel, Proofreader; Tim Griffin/IndexServ, Indexer; Olivia Nellums, Fact Checker; Dawn Friedman, Photo Researcher; Linda S. Koutris, Photo Selector

Original cover art by Todd Marshall

The Design Lab: Kathleen Petelinsek, Design; Kari Thornborough, Page Production

Library of Congress Cataloging-in-Publication Data
Gray, Susan Heinrichs.
  Crinoids and Blastoids / by Susan H. Gray.
    p. cm. — (Exploring dinosaurs & prehistoric creatures)
  Includes index.
  ISBN 1-59296-365-X (lib. bound : alk. paper)
  1. Crinoidea, Fossil—Juvenile literature. 2. Blastoidea—Juvenile literature. I. Title. II. Series: Gray, Susan Heinrichs. Exploring dinosaurs & prehistoric creatures.
  QE782.G73 2005
  563'.92—dc22   2004018060

Table of Contents

CHAPTER ONE

A ROUGH TIME

The storm grew more violent every minute. Dark clouds swirled overhead. Strong winds whipped across the ocean's surface. Huge waves rose and fell, making great crashing sounds. Even beneath the surface, the water surged this way and that. Fine silt from the seafloor was churned up, making the water cloudy. Flat, many-legged creatures called trilobites (TRY-lo-bites) scuttled into the sand for protection.

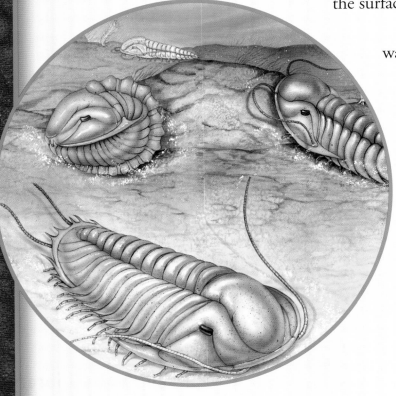

Trilobites once scurried along the ocean floor. These prehistoric creatures lived long before dinosaurs existed.

Hundreds of crinoids (KRY-noidz) and blastoids (BLASS-toidz) swayed stiffly in the water. Their **flimsy** arms could do nothing against the water's movements. Although the animals were firmly anchored to the seafloor, the storm was too strong for some of them. A few of the animals were thrown over on their sides.

Crinoids still exist today, although a greater variety filled the seas in prehistoric times.

A few more were uprooted and floated away. Most, however, held their ground.

Although crinoids are sea animals, they look more like colorful underwater plants.

In time, the storm passed and the sea grew calm again. The sand

settled, and the water became clear. Trilobites ventured out from their

burrows. The crinoids and blastoids straightened up, spread their arms,

and began to feed. Life returned to normal.

CHAPTER TWO

WHAT ARE CRINOIDS?

Crinoids are sea animals that have existed on Earth for the past 490 million years. Thousands of different kinds have become **extinct,** but several hundred kinds still exist today.

Most crinoids of the past looked like tall flowers with roots, long stems, and delicate petals. They were not plants, however. They were animals that moved and gathered food.

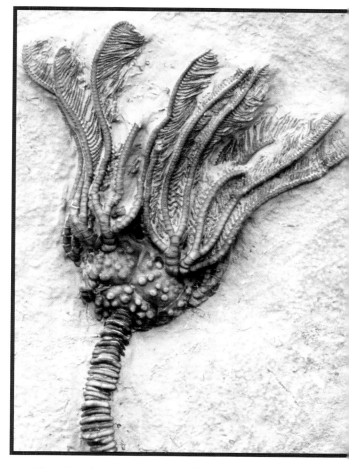

Not all prehistoric animals had scales and sharp teeth! Plantlike crinoids had stems, roots, and petals.

The main part of the crinoid's body was a small cup called the calyx (KAY-liks). The calyx was usually no more than 1 inch (2.5 centimeters) tall and was about the size of a grape. The outside of the calyx was covered with many small, hard plates. These protected the

Certain prehistoric creatures left very few traces of their lives on Earth, but crinoid fossils are plentiful and easy to find.

stomach and the other organs inside.

Reaching up from the cup were arm-like structures that gathered food.

Some crinoids had long, feathery arms. Others had

A crinoid's stem stretched between its calyx and the ocean floor.

plate-covered arms with many branches. The arms swept small

particles of food toward the top of the calyx, where the crinoid's

mouth was located.

A long stem called the column extended down from the calyx

to the seafloor below. There, the column spread out and attached to the floor. Some crinoids had complex, rootlike systems for attaching. Some crinoids had hooks at the bottom of their columns. These hooks helped them cling to corals or other hard objects. On some crinoids, the bottom of the column spread out into a plate that became glued to a rock or a shell. Still other crinoids had hairlike structures growing out from the column. These crinoids would wrap those structures around hard objects to anchor themselves in place.

Crinoid stems were very complex. They were made of hundreds of small, button-shaped disks, stacked one on top of the other. The disks interlocked and fit snugly together. This tight fit made the crinoid columns rather stiff and unable to bend very far.

Columns often reached several feet in length, holding the little animals' bodies well above the ocean floor. A tunnel ran the whole length of the column, from the cup down to the crinoid's anchor.

Food moved down this tunnel, helping to nourish the animal's

disks and anchoring system.

A living crinoid anchors itself to a piece of coral.

CHAPTER THREE

WHAT ARE BLASTOIDS?

Blastoids are animals that lived in the ocean from about 430 million to 250 million years ago. They were related to crinoids but have become extinct.

In some ways, blastoids looked very much like crinoids. A hard cup less than 1 inch (2.5 cm) tall protected the blastoid's organs. Arms reached upward from the cup and swept food toward the

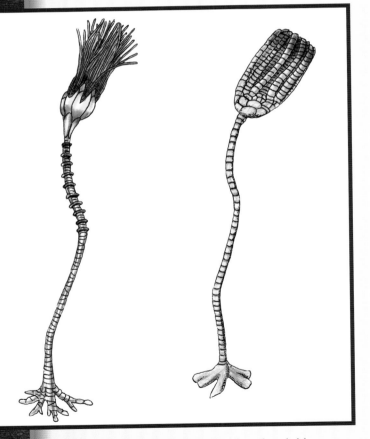

Crinoids and blastoids were similar, but they did have some important differences. Can you see some differences between the blastoid (left) and the crinoid (right) in this illustration?

mouth. The cup sat atop

a column made of little disks.

The bottom of the column

was attached to the seafloor.

Food moved down a passage-

way in the column and nour-

ished the different body parts.

There were also some

important differences between

blastoids and crinoids.

Blastoid arms were arranged

in five rows along the out-

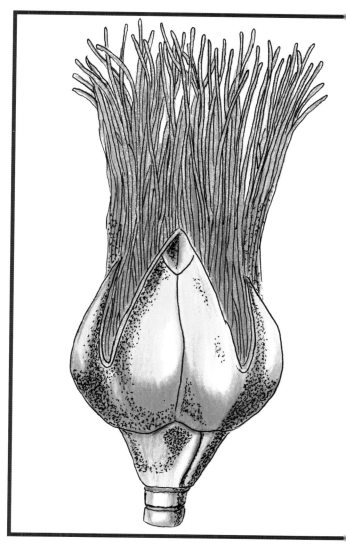

The arms of a blastoid were arranged in five groups, or rows, on the outside of its cup.

side of the cup. The arms were delicate and did not have plate-

covered branches.

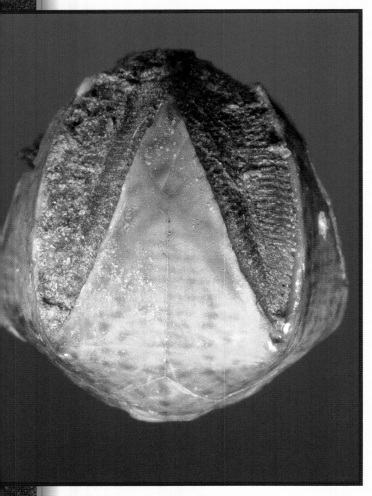

Blastoid fossils often reveal how the animal's plates held together after it died.

At the very top of the cup, blastoids had six tiny openings. The smallest opening was the blastoid's mouth, and the other five openings encircled it. Four of the five holes surrounding the mouth were for breathing and one was for **ejecting** waste.

The plates of a blastoid's cup were fused together. A crinoid's plates were held in place by soft tissues. When a crinoid died, the plates of its cup usually fell apart. When a blastoid died, its plates often held together.

CHAPTER FOUR

HOW ARE BLASTOIDS AND CRINOIDS RELATED?

Blastoids and crinoids belong to a large group of animals called the echinoderms (ih-KY-nuh-durmz). The name *echinoderm* comes from Greek words that mean "spiny skin."

Echinoderms include not only animals of past times, but also many

About 700 types of sea urchins live in Earth's oceans today. The spines on these spiky echinoderms are often poisonous.

modern animals such as sea stars, sand dollars, and sea urchins. Both **ancient** and modern forms are known for their rough or spiny body parts.

Echinoderms have always lived in the ocean. They have never lived on land, in lakes, or in streams. Their bodies usually do not have an obvious right side and left side. Instead, they are rounded or have parts sticking out from a round center. The body is divided into five parts. In some echinoderms, such as sea stars and sand dollars, the five parts are easy to see. In others, such as sea urchins, the five parts are hidden by spines.

Crinoids and blastoids, like other echinoderms, have lived only in the oceans. Their cups were round in shape and their body parts were arranged in fives. Blastoids had arms lined up in five rows. Crinoids of the past and present have had five arms or five sets of

If a sea star loses one of its five arms, it is able to grow a new one!

arms. In some crinoids, the tunnel inside the column is shaped like

a five-pointed star.

Paleontologists (PAY-lee-uhn-TOL-uh-jists) are scientists who

study ancient plants and animals. They look at echinoderms from long ago. They tell us that these animals have been around for at least 540 million years. So far, we know of about 19,000 different kinds of echinoderms, and most of them have become extinct. All of the blastoids and most of the crinoids are among those that died out long ago.

A paleontologist measures a fish fossil. Scientists rely on fossils to tell them when and where prehistoric animals lived. Sometimes they can even use fossils to determine how fast a creature moved or whether it lived alone or in a group.

CRINOIDS OF TODAY

Many people believe that all crinoids died out millions of years ago. This is not the case. Crinoids still live in the oceans. While some are found at depths of up to 1,000 feet (305 meters), many others live in much shallower waters. Some modern crinoids have stalks just as their ancestors did. They are called sea lilies. Others have no stalks and creep about or cling to the seafloor with long, hooked structures. These animals are called feather stars.

Sea lilies and feather stars are beautiful animals that are not often seen by humans. Yet in some places, the seafloor is covered with them. Paleontologists are interested in these modern crinoids. They study the living animals so they can better understand how the extinct crinoids might have lived.

For example, scientists might wonder whether ancient sea creatures ate crinoids. Their cups and columns were hard and probably not very tasty. But their arms may have been soft and tender. Scientists studying modern sea lilies and feather stars have found that fish usually leave the crinoids' hard, crunchy parts alone. However, they sometimes nibble on those soft arms. This usually doesn't kill the sea lilies or feather stars. They just grow their arms back. Paleontologists think that the same thing happened to the crinoids of long ago.

CHAPTER FIVE

WHAT DID BLASTOIDS AND CRINOIDS DO ALL DAY?

A nimals that are anchored to the seafloor can't do a whole lot,

so blastoids and crinoids probably spent much of their time

just eating small food particles that drifted by. Perhaps these animals

lived where water currents were strong enough to

bring a steady flow of such particles.

Food probably included

little pieces of algae, micro-

scopic animals, and

even pieces of dead sea

creatures. Once a food

particle touched the

crinoid or blastoid arm,

Plankton are microscopic animals that float along ocean currents. Crinoids and blastoids once fed on these tiny creatures.

A modern-day crinoid uses its feathery arms to gather food in the Great Barrier Reef.

tiny, fingerlike structures on the arm swept the food toward the mouth. The ancient echinoderms did not reach out and grab food, but ate small pieces of matter that came to them. Grains of sand were sometimes taken in with all the other food, and the animals would send them out again through a hole on top of the calyx.

Most, but not all, blastoids and crinoids spent their lives attached to the seafloor. Some crinoids had no stalk at all. They had only a calyx and arms. These crinoids may have been able to swim in short bursts or to float on the surface. They could not chase down **prey,** however, or swim long distances.

WHEN THINGS GET BORING

Have you ever walked along the beach collecting seashells? If you have, you've probably found shells with little holes in them. The holes are perfectly round and look as if they were made by tiny drills.

Snails called boring snails or drilling snails made the holes. To make a hole, a snail crawls onto the shell of a living animal. It dabs a chemical on the shell, causing the shell to dissolve. As the shell dissolves, the snail runs its rough tongue over the area. By doing this over and over, the snail bores a hole into the shell. In time, it reaches the animal inside. Then the snail survives by stealing the other animal's food. A seashell with a hole in it probably belonged to an animal that had lived with a drilling snail for a long time.

This is not something that happens only with modern animals. Scientists believe that it also took

place millions of years ago. Paleontologists have found blastoid and crinoid fossils with similar holes. This means that even in ancient times, echinoderms had to put up with other animals drilling into them.

There is one big mystery, however. Drilling snails did not exist until about 110 million years ago. The blastoid and crinoid fossils with holes are much older than that. So what sort of animal bored those holes? Were there other drilling animals we don't know about yet? Could the holes be a sign of disease? Did something cause the holes to appear after the crinoids and blastoids died? Many questions remain.

CHAPTER SIX

WHAT HAPPENED TO THE CRINOIDS AND BLASTOIDS?

When something causes many different kinds of plants and animals to die out, the result is called a mass extinction. Paleontologists tell us that there have been five major mass extinctions since life first appeared on Earth. They say that there also have been some minor mass extinctions.

Scientists believe that a huge mass extinction wiped out most of the crinoids and all of the blastoids about 250 million years ago. This was the biggest mass extinction ever.

Scientists think an asteroid may have hit Earth and caused a mass extinction about 250 million years ago. Several million years later, another mass extinction occurred that killed off all the dinosaurs.

Plants and animals across the land died by the millions. Almost all of the sea creatures disappeared as well. Only a few kinds of crinoids made it through, but not a single blastoid survived. Some scientists call the event the Great Dying.

Paleontologists are not certain what triggered such disasters. Perhaps volcanoes were the cause. They may have **spewed** gas and ash into the air, darkening the skies and killing plants and animals. Maybe an asteroid collided with Earth, sending poisonous materials everywhere. Perhaps volcanoes and asteroids are *both* to blame.

Mass extinctions did not happen overnight. Sometimes it took years for plants to waste away. Then the animals that fed on those plants slowly died out. And the animals that fed on *them* were the next to vanish. Over time, all living things that could not adapt to the changing Earth disappeared.

New life-forms always arose after mass extinctions. As blastoids

and crinoids died 250 million years ago, they tumbled to the seafloor.

Sand settled over their bodies, and they became fossils. But about

20 million years later, some new animals walked along the shore.

They were small, four-legged creatures—the first dinosaurs.

Dinosaurs existed for nearly 183 million years.

Glossary

ancient (AYN-shunt) Something that is ancient is very old; from millions of years ago. Paleontologists study ancient life.

dissolve (di-ZOLV) To dissolve means to melt away or disappear upon coming in contact with a liquid. A boring snail dabs a chemical on a shell, causing the shell to dissolve.

ejecting (i-JEKT-ing) Ejecting is sending or shooting something out forcefully. One opening in the blastoid's cup was for ejecting waste materials.

extinct (ek-STINGKT) A plant or animal that has died out is extinct. Blastoids are now extinct.

flimsy (FLIM-zee) Something that is flimsy is weak and easily damaged. The crinoids' flimsy arms could do nothing against the water's movements.

prey (PRAY) Animals that are hunted and eaten by others are called prey. Blastoids and crinoids could not chase down prey.

spewed (SPEWD) Something sent out in a violent gush or flood is spewed. Volcanoes may have spewed gas and ash into the air, darkening skies and killing plants and animals.

Did You Know?

▸ Some Native Americans strung together pieces of crinoid columns to make necklaces.

▸ Blastoid fossils are often mistakenly thought to be fossilized hickory nuts or strawberries.

▸ The anchoring system of a blastoid or crinoid is sometimes called its holdfast.

▸ Crinoid stems are among the most common fossils in the world. People find them along roadsides, on mountains and bluffs, in streambeds, and in backyards.

▸ The longest crinoid stems were about 75 feet (23 m) long and are believed to have been attached to driftwood.

How to Learn More

AT THE LIBRARY

Blaxland, Beth. *Sea Stars, Sea Urchins, and Their Relatives: Echinoderms.*
Philadelphia: Chelsea House Publishers, 2003.

Cefrey, Holly. *Fossils.* New York: PowerKids Press, 2003.

Lambert, David, Darren Naish, and Liz Wyse. *Dinosaur Encyclopedia.* New York: DK Publishing, 2001.

ON THE WEB

Visit our home page for lots of links about crinoids and blastoids:
http://www.childsworld.com/links.html
NOTE TO PARENTS, TEACHERS, AND LIBRARIANS: We routinely verify our Web links
to make sure they're safe, active sites—so encourage your readers to check them out!

PLACES TO VISIT OR CONTACT

AMERICAN MUSEUM OF NATURAL HISTORY
*To view numerous fossils of dinosaurs and other
prehistoric creatures*
Central Park West at 79th Street
New York, NY 10024-5192
212/769-5100

CARNEGIE MUSEUM OF NATURAL HISTORY
*To view a variety of dinosaur skeletons, as well
as fossils of other extinct animals*
4400 Forbes Avenue
Pittsburgh, PA 15213
412/622-3131

FIELD MUSEUM OF NATURAL HISTORY
*To find out more about how fossils of prehistoric animals
are prepared for scientific study*
1400 South Lake Shore Drive
Chicago, IL 60605-2496
312/922-9410

MONTEREY BAY AQUARIUM
To see living specimens of echinoderms
886 Cannery Row
Monterey, CA 93940
831/648-4888

SMITHSONIAN NATIONAL MUSEUM
OF NATURAL HISTORY
*To learn more about fossils and the evolution of modern
animals and plants from their prehistoric ancestors*
10th Street and Constitution Avenue NW
Washington, DC 20560-0166
202/357-270045

The Geologic Time Scale

CAMBRIAN PERIOD

Date: 540 million to 505 million years ago
Most major animal groups appeared by the end of this period. Trilobites were common and algae became more diversified.

ORDOVICIAN PERIOD

Date: 505 million to 440 million years ago
Marine life became more diversified. Crinoids and blastoids appeared, as did corals and primitive fish. The first land plants appeared. The climate changed greatly during this period—it began as warm and moist, but temperatures ultimately dropped. Huge glaciers formed, causing sea levels to fall.

SILURIAN PERIOD

Date: 440 million to 410 million years ago Glaciers melted, sea levels rose, and Earth's climate became more stable. Plants with vascular systems developed. This means they had parts that helped them to conduct food and water.

DEVONIAN PERIOD

Date: 410 million to 360 million years ago
Fish became more diverse, as did land plants. The first trees and forests appeared at this time, and the earliest seed-bearing plants began to grow. The first land-living vertebrates and insects appeared. Fossils also reveal evidence of the first ammonoids and amphibians. The climate was warm and mild.

CARBONIFEROUS PERIOD

Date: 360 million to 286 million years ago
The climate was warm and humid, but cooled toward the end of the period. Coal swamps dotted the landscape, as did a multitude of ferns. The earliest reptiles existed. Pelycosaurs such as *Edaphosaurus* evolved toward the end of the Carboniferous period.

PERMIAN PERIOD

Date: 286 million to 248 million years ago
Algae, sponges, and corals were common on the ocean floor. Amphibians and reptiles were also prevalent at this time, as were seed-bearing plants and conifers. This period ended with the largest mass extinction on Earth. This may have been caused by volcanic activity or the formation of glaciers and the lowering of sea levels.

TRIASSIC PERIOD

Date: 248 million to 208 million years ago
The climate during this period was warm and dry. The first true mammals appeared, as did frogs, salamanders, and lizards. Evergreen trees made up much of the plant life. The first dinosaurs, including *Coelophysis*, existed. In the skies, pterosaurs became the earliest winged reptiles to take flight. In the seas, ichthyosaurs and plesiosaurs made their appearance.

JURASSIC PERIOD

Date: 208 million to 144 million years ago
The climate of the Jurassic period was warm
and moist. The first birds appeared at this
time, and plant life was more diverse and
widespread. Although dinosaurs didn't even
exist in the beginning of the Triassic period,
they ruled Earth by Jurassic times. *Allosaurus,
Apatosaurus, Archaeopteryx, Brachiosaurus,
Compsognathus, Diplodocus, Ichthyosaurus,
Plesiosaurus,* and *Stegosaurus* were just a few
of the prehistoric creatures that lived during
this period.

CRETACEOUS PERIOD

Date: 144 million to 65 million years ago
The climate of the Cretaceous period was
fairly mild. Many modern plants developed,
including those with flowers. With flowering
plants came a greater diversity of insect life.
Birds further developed into two types: flying
and flightless. Prehistoric creatures such as
*Ankylosaurus, Edmontosaurus, Iguanodon,
Maiasaura, Oviraptor, Psittacosaurus, Spinos-
aurus, Triceratops, Troodon, Tyrannosaurus
rex,* and *Velociraptor* all existed during this
period. At the end of the Cretaceous period
came a great mass extinction that wiped out
the dinosaurs, along with many other groups
of animals.

TERTIARY PERIOD

Date: 65 million to 1.8 million years ago
Mammals were extremely diversified at this
time, and modern-day creatures such as horses,
dogs, cats, bears, and whales developed.

QUATERNARY PERIOD

Date: 1.8 million years ago to today
Temperatures continued to drop during this
period. Several periods of glacial development
led to what is known as the Ice Age.
Prehistoric creatures such as glyptodonts,
mammoths, mastodons, *Megatherium,* and
saber-toothed cats roamed the land. A mass
extinction of these animals occurred approxi-
mately 10,000 years ago. The first human
beings evolved during the Quaternary period.

Index

About the Author

Susan H. Gray has bachelor's and master's degrees in zoology and has taught college-level courses in biology. She first fell in love with fossil hunting while studying paleontology in college. In her 25 years as an author, she has written many articles for scientists and researchers, and many science books for children. Susan enjoys gardening, traveling, and playing the piano. She and her husband, Michael, live in Cabot, Arkansas.